Preface

Welcome to the CTET PAPER 2 CLASS VI TO VIII LANGUAGE 1 Book!

Teaching is a journey of learning, discovery, and personal growth. This book is designed to support you on that journey as you prepare for the Central Teacher Eligibility Test (CTET). Whether you are an aspiring educator or looking to enhance your knowledge, this book will equip you with essential concepts, strategies, and insights to excel in the exam and in your future teaching career.

Our goal is to make your learning experience meaningful and effective. Each chapter in this book has been carefully crafted to engage both your curiosity and critical thinking, covering core topics essential for the CTET exam. Along the way, you will find opportunities to reflect on best practices in education, the role of teachers in shaping society, and the importance of fostering an inclusive and supportive learning environment.

Table of Contents

Chapter 1: Questions

1. What is the primary goal of teaching reading comprehension?

a) To enhance memorisation skills

b) To develop critical thinking and understanding

c) To teach vocabulary in isolation

d) To test grammar knowledge

Answer: b) To develop critical thinking and understanding

2. Which is the best strategy for teaching vocabulary in context?

a) Memorizing word lists

b) Using words from reading passages in discussions

c) Focusing only on dictionary definitions

d) Teaching vocabulary unrelated to reading

Answer: b) Using words from reading passages in discussions

3. What does the term "remedial teaching" refer to?

a) Teaching advanced students

b) Providing extra help to students with learning difficulties

c) Preparing students for competitive exams

d) Giving homework assignments

Answer: b) Providing extra help to students with learning difficulties

4. Which of the following is an example of a language acquisition activity?

a) Grammar worksheets

b) Engaging in conversations

c) Filling in blanks with word choices

d) Memorizing parts of speech

Answer: b) Engaging in conversations

5. What is a crucial principle of language teaching?

a) Language is best learned through passive listening

b) Language learning requires active interaction

c) Language is acquired through rote memorisation

d) Language should be taught only through grammar drills

Answer: b) Language learning requires active interaction

6. Which skill is developed through reading poetry?

a) Identifying scientific terms

b) Understanding rhythm and figurative language

c) Memorizing grammar rules

d) Improving factual recall

Answer: b) Understanding rhythm and figurative language

6. What is the primary purpose of listening activities in language teaching?

a) To improve grammar

b) To develop comprehension and attention skills

c) To memorise vocabulary

d) To practice spelling

Answer: b) To develop comprehension and attention skills

7. Which material is most suitable for evaluating language proficiency?

a) A multiple-choice grammar test

b) A short essay on a familiar topic

c) A science textbook

d) A mathematical puzzle

Answer: b) A short essay on a familiar topic

8. How can teachers address language teaching challenges in a diverse classroom?

a) By giving identical tasks to all students

b) By incorporating culturally relevant content

c) By ignoring language diversity

d) By focusing only on advanced students

Answer: b) By incorporating culturally relevant content

9. What is the role of speaking activities in language development?

a) To help students apply grammar rules

b) To improve students' pronunciation and communication

c) To memorise spelling patterns

d) To complete textbook exercises

Answer: b) To improve students' pronunciation and communication

10. Which method promotes language acquisition?

a) Using real-life communication scenarios

b) Giving only grammar-focused assignments

c) Avoiding speaking activities

d) Memorizing vocabulary lists

Answer: a) Using real-life communication scenarios

11. What is the purpose of remedial teaching in language learning?

a) To prepare students for exams only

b) To address learning gaps and difficulties

c) To teach new concepts

d) To replace classroom teaching

Answer: b) To address learning gaps and difficulties

12. Which of the following is an essential language skill?

a) Listening, speaking, reading, and writing

b) Memorizing grammar rules

c) Practicing mathematical equations

d) Solving puzzles

Answer: a) Listening, speaking, reading, and writing

13. How can teachers evaluate reading comprehension effectively?

a) By asking students to recall facts only

b) By assessing students' understanding of main ideas and inferences

c) By focusing solely on grammar

d) By giving spelling tests

Answer: b) By assessing students' understanding of main ideas and inferences

14. Which teaching-learning material helps develop language skills?

a) Picture books and storybooks

b) Mathematical models

c) Chemistry lab equipment

d) Geography maps

Answer: a) Picture books and storybooks

15. What is the importance of teaching drama in language classes?

a) It improves students' math skills

b) It develops communication and expression

c) It focuses only on writing skills

d) It replaces classroom discussions

Answer: b) It develops communication and expression

16. What challenges are common in language teaching in a diverse classroom?

a) Language barriers and varying proficiency levels

b) Lack of physical education classes

c) Too much focus on art activities

d) Students having identical language abilities

Answer: a) Language barriers and varying proficiency levels

17. What is a suitable activity for teaching listening skills?

a) Storytelling sessions

b) Silent reading

c) Writing essays

d) Solving math problems

Answer: a) Storytelling sessions

18. Which strategy promotes active language acquisition?

a) Engaging in role-play activities

b) Reading silently without discussion

c) Memorizing grammar rules

d) Practicing only written exercises

Answer: a)Engaging in role-play activities

19. How can teachers support students with language learning difficulties?

a) By providing individualised instruction and feedback

b) By ignoring their struggles

c) By assigning the same tasks to everyone

d) By focusing only on advanced students

Answer: a) By providing individualised instruction and feedback

20. What is the role of comprehension passages in language learning?

a) To improve understanding of texts

b) To memorise grammar rules

c) To develop mathematical reasoning

d) To replace speaking activities

Answer: a) To improve understanding of texts

21. Which strategy helps students learn new vocabulary?

a) Contextual usage through reading and conversation

b) Memorizing lists without practice

c) Focusing only on spelling

d) Ignoring unknown words

Answer: a) Contextual usage through reading and conversation

22. What is the main focus of the pedagogy of language development?

a) Facilitating communication and comprehension

b) Teaching only grammar rules

c) Avoiding oral language activities

d) Limiting instruction to textbooks

Answer: a) Facilitating communication and comprehension

23. How does learning in a second language differ from acquisition?

a) Learning is formal and explicit, while acquisition is natural and unconscious

b) Learning happens without any instruction

c) Acquisition requires grammar-focused teaching

d) There is no difference between the two

Answer: a) Learning is formal and explicit, while acquisition is natural and unconscious

24. What role does writing play in language development?

a) It reinforces communication and thinking skills

b) It replaces oral communication

c) It focuses only on spelling

d) It is unrelated to reading comprehension

Answer: a) It reinforces communication and thinking skills

25. Which of the following characteristics of an effective language teacher?

a) Ability to create engaging, interactive lessons

b) Focus on only one language skill

c) Avoiding student questions

d) Relying solely on textbooks

Answer: a) Ability to create engaging, interactive lessons

26. What is the primary goal of remedial teaching in language?

a) To address gaps in learning

b) To teach new advanced concepts

c) To replace regular teaching

d) To eliminate classroom discussions

Answer: a) To address gaps in learning

27. Which type of passage requires students to analyse emotions and tone?

a) Poetry

b) Mathematical problems

c) Instruction manuals

d) Science articles

Answer: a) Poetry

28. How can teachers assess speaking skills?

a) Through role-plays and presentations

b) By assigning written essays only

c) By giving spelling tests

d) By focusing only on grammar drills

Answer: a) Through role-plays and presentations

29. What is the purpose of using drama in language teaching?

a) To improve fluency and self-expression

b) To focus only on grammar

c) To teach scientific facts

d) To replace creative activities

Answer: a) To improve fluency and self-expression

30. Which skill is crucial for developing reading comprehension?

a) Identifying the main idea and supporting details

b) Memorizing word meanings without context

c) Ignoring the structure of texts

d) Focusing only on spelling

Answer: a) Identifying the main idea and supporting details

31. What role does listening play in language acquisition?

a) It develops understanding and pronunciation

b) It replaces written tasks

c) It discourages student interaction

d) It limits student engagement

Answer: a) It develops understanding and pronunciation

32. What is the main challenge in teaching language to students from diverse backgrounds?

a) Different language proficiency levels among students

b) Lack of interest in any subject

c) Identical cultural experiences

d) Uniform learning styles

Answer: a) Different language proficiency levels among students

33. How can teachers address students with varied language proficiency?

a) By using differentiated teaching strategies

b) By giving identical tasks to all students

c) By ignoring students with difficulties

d) By only teaching advanced students

Answer: a) By using differentiated teaching strategies

34. What is a critical aspect of evaluating language comprehension?

a) Assessing both accuracy and fluency

b) Focusing only on grammar

c) Ignoring oral skills

d) Testing only vocabulary

Answer: a) Assessing both accuracy and fluency

35. Which strategy is effective for teaching a new language?

a) Integrating listening, speaking, reading, and writing activities

b) Relying only on grammar-based instruction

c) Avoiding group activities

d) Teaching isolated vocabulary

Answer: a) Integrating listening, speaking, reading, and writing activities

36. What type of reading material can help build comprehension skills?

a) Stories with familiar themes

b) Scientific manuals

c) Complex mathematical texts

d) Technical reports

Answer: a) Stories with familiar themes

37. What is the importance of using teaching-learning materials in language classes?

a) They make learning more engaging and meaningful

b) They focus only on memorisation

c) They eliminate the need for discussions

d) They discourage student interaction

Answer: a) They make learning more engaging and meaningful

38. Which of the following helps evaluate listening comprehension?

a) Asking students to summarise a story they heard

b) Assigning only grammar worksheets

c) Testing vocabulary in isolation

d) Focusing solely on written assessments

Answer: a) Asking students to summarise a story they heard

39. How can teachers help students improve their writing skills?

a) By giving them meaningful prompts to write about

b) By focusing only on grammar corrections

c) By assigning repetitive spelling tests

d) By discouraging creative expression

Answer: a) By giving them meaningful prompts to write about

40. What is an effective way to teach pronunciation?

a) Through listening and repeating exercises

b) By focusing only on reading activities

c) By ignoring spoken language

d) By teaching spelling patterns exclusively

Answer: a) Through listening and repeating exercises

41. How can teachers use role-play to teach language?

a) By simulating real-life conversations

b) By focusing only on grammar rules

c) By avoiding speaking activities

d) By assigning repetitive worksheets

Answer: a) By simulating real-life conversations

42. What is the role of feedback in language learning?

a) It helps students improve and refine their language skills

b) It discourages participation

c) It focuses only on mistakes

d) It eliminates the need for practice

Answer: a) It helps students improve and refine their language skills

43. Which activity helps students practice speaking skills?

a) Group discussions on familiar topics

b) Silent reading sessions

c) Spelling drills

d) Grammar exercises only

Answer: a) Group discussions on familiar topics

44. What is the purpose of remedial teaching?

a) To address gaps in students' understanding and performance

b) To provide extra homework

c) To teach only advanced content

d) To prepare students for competitive exams

Answer: a) To address gaps in students' understanding and performance

45. How can teachers create an inclusive language classroom?

a) By valuing and incorporating students' cultural backgrounds

b) By assigning the same tasks to everyone

c) By ignoring language diversity

d) By focusing only on written work

Answer: a) By valuing and incorporating students' cultural backgrounds

46. Which technique helps in developing listening skills?

a) Playing audio stories and discussing them

b) Assigning only written assignments

c) Conducting silent reading sessions

d) Ignoring oral language activities

Answer: a) Playing audio stories and discussing them

47. How can teachers evaluate reading comprehension effectively?

a) By asking students to identify themes and main ideas

b) By focusing only on vocabulary tests

c) By giving only factual questions

d) By assigning spelling corrections

Answer: a) By asking students to identify themes and central ideas

48. What is the benefit of using poetry in language teaching?

a) It enhances appreciation for language and rhythm

b) It focuses only on grammar structures

c) It discourages creative thinking

d) It limits vocabulary development

Answer: a) It enhances appreciation for language and rhythm

49. How does remedial teaching support struggling learners?

a) By providing targeted support based on individual needs

b) By giving additional homework

c) By ignoring their difficulties

d) By preparing students for competitive exams

Answer: a) By providing targeted support based on individual needs

50. What is the most effective way to teach language to young learners?

a) Through interactive games and storytelling

b) By focusing only on grammar drills

c) By giving long lectures

d) By avoiding spoken language

Answer: a) Through interactive games and storytelling

51. How can teachers evaluate speaking skills in students?

a) By conducting oral presentations and role-plays

b) By focusing only on written assignments

c) By assigning grammar worksheets

d) By giving multiple-choice tests

Answer: a) By conducting oral presentations and role-plays

52. Which method promotes active listening?

a) Listening to a story and answering questions about it

b) Copying sentences from the board

c) Memorizing word lists

d) Reading silently without discussion

Answer: a) Listening to a story and answering questions about it

53. What is the purpose of comprehension questions after reading?

a) To assess students' understanding of the text

b) To test their spelling ability

c) To practice only grammar rules

d) To complete worksheets

Answer: a) To assess students' understanding of the text

54. How can teachers address language difficulties in a diverse classroom?

a) By using differentiated tasks and scaffolding

b) By teaching all students the same way

c) By avoiding group work

d) By focusing only on fluent speakers

Answer: a) By using differentiated tasks and scaffolding

55. Which skill is developed by group discussions in language learning?

a) Speaking and critical thinking skills

b) Memorizing spelling rules

c) Writing formal essays

d) Identifying grammar errors

Answer: a) Speaking and critical thinking skills

56. What is the challenge of teaching language in multilingual classrooms?

a) Students may have varying levels of proficiency

b) All students learn at the same pace

c) Students do not need additional support

d) Language diversity makes teaching easier

Answer: a) Students may have varying levels of proficiency

57. Which is an example of a listening activity?

a) Students listen to a song and discuss the lyrics

b) Writing essays without discussion

c) Practicing spelling lists

d) Memorizing grammar rules

Answer: a) Students listen to a song and discuss the lyrics

58. How can teachers promote reading comprehension?

a) By encouraging students to summarise what they read

b) By assigning only factual recall questions

c) By avoiding discussions about the text

d) By giving long lists of vocabulary words

Answer: a) By encouraging students to summarise what they read

59. What is the purpose of remedial teaching?

a) To provide extra support for students facing difficulties

b) To focus only on advanced learners

c) To assign additional homework

d) To eliminate discussions from class

Answer: a) To provide extra support for students facing difficulties

60. What does scaffolding in language teaching mean?

a) Providing support and gradually reducing it as students become independent

b) Avoiding challenging tasks

c) Focusing only on written activities

d) Giving answers directly to students

Answer: a) Providing support and gradually reducing it as students become independent

61. How can teachers assess listening comprehension?

a) By asking students to retell what they heard

b) By giving only grammar tests

c) By assigning silent reading tasks

d) By focusing only on spelling

Answer: a) By asking students to retell what they heard

62. Which activity helps develop vocabulary naturally?

a) Conversations in real-life situations

b) Memorizing word definitions

c) Practicing spelling drills

d) Writing long grammar exercises

Answer: a) Conversations in real-life situations

63. How does role-play benefit language learners?

a) It helps students practice communication in real contexts

b) It replaces written assessments

c) It focuses only on pronunciation

d) It discourages collaboration

Answer: a) It helps students practice communication in real contexts

64. What is the main goal of teaching poetry?

a) To develop an appreciation for language, rhythm, and imagery

b) To teach grammar rules

c) To replace prose reading

d) To memorise lines for exams

Answer: a) To develop an appreciation for language, rhythm, and imagery

66. What is a challenge in teaching language to students with different abilities?

a) Varying levels of language proficiency

b) Uniform pace of learning

c) Identical learning preferences

d) No need for individualised support

Answer: a) Varying levels of language proficiency

67. How can teachers enhance writing skills?

a) By providing meaningful topics for students to write about

b) By assigning only grammar exercises

c) By avoiding creative tasks

d) By focusing only on handwriting

Answer: a) By providing meaningful topics for students to write about

68. What is the best way to improve speaking skills?

a) Engaging students in group discussions and presentations

b) Assigning only written tasks

c) Giving vocabulary lists to memorise

d) Avoiding spoken activities

Answer: a) Engaging students in group discussions and presentations

69. Which activity promotes listening comprehension?

a) Listening to a conversation and answering related questions

b) Copying notes from the board

c) Memorizing vocabulary

d) Writing essays only

Answer: a) Listening to a conversation and answering related questions

70. What is the purpose of remedial language teaching?

a) To address gaps in students' understanding and skills

b) To prepare students for competitive exams

c) To give extra homework

d) To replace regular instruction

Answer: a) To address gaps in students' understanding and skills

71. What is an effective strategy to teach students with diverse language backgrounds?

a) Using multilingual support and visual aids

b) Giving identical tasks to all students

c) Ignoring cultural differences

d) Focusing only on fluent speakers

Answer: a) Using multilingual support and visual aids

72. How does reading drama benefit students?

a) It improves expression and fluency

b) It replaces academic subjects

c) It focuses only on grammar

d) It discourages creativity

Answer: a) It improves expression and fluency

73. What is the role of feedback in language development?

a) To guide students toward improvement

b) To discourage student effort

c) To avoid corrections

d) To limit student participation

Answer: a) To guide students toward improvement

74. How can teachers help students struggling with pronunciation?

a) By using listening and repetition activities

b) By avoiding spoken language

c) By focusing only on grammar

d) By giving spelling tests

Answer: a) By using listening and repetition activities

75. What is the benefit of group discussions?

a) They promote speaking skills and critical thinking

b) They eliminate individual accountability

c) They focus only on written work

d) They limit collaboration

Answer: a) They promote speaking skills and critical thinking

76. What is a common challenge in evaluating language proficiency?

a) Balancing assessments of all four language skills

b) Focusing only on listening skills

c) Giving only vocabulary tests

d) Avoiding student feedback

Answer: a) Balancing assessments of all four language skills

77. Which teaching strategy promotes active learning?

a) Encouraging students to ask questions and participate actively

b) Giving long lectures without interaction

c) Focusing only on note-taking

d) Avoiding classroom discussions

Answer: a) Encouraging students to ask questions and participate actively

78. How can teachers foster independent learning in language?

a) By encouraging students to explore topics on their own

b) By giving all answers directly

c) By discouraging questions

d) By avoiding creative tasks

Answer: a) By encouraging students to explore topics on their own

79. Which activity enhances listening skills?

a) Storytelling sessions with follow-up questions

b) Copying words from the board

c) Memorizing spelling lists

d) Writing essays only

Answer: a) Storytelling sessions with follow-up questions

80.How can teachers promote creative writing?

a) By providing prompts that inspire imagination

b) By focusing only on factual writing

c) By avoiding storytelling activities

d) By limiting feedback

Answer: a) By providing prompts that inspire imagination

81. What is an effective way to teach grammar in context?

a) Using stories or dialogues that naturally include grammar rules

b) Giving isolated grammar worksheets

c) Avoiding grammar lessons altogether

d) Teaching only through textbook exercises

Answer: a) Using stories or dialogues that naturally include grammar rules

82. How does peer learning benefit language development?

a) It encourages collaboration and active participation

b) It discourages group interaction

c) It focuses only on competition

d) It limits student involvement

Answer: a) It encourages collaboration and active participation

83. What is the role of visual aids in language teaching?

a) They help explain new vocabulary and concepts

b) They discourage student interaction

c) They replace spoken language

d) They limit creativity

Answer: a) They help explain new vocabulary and concepts

84. Which activity can improve reading fluency?

a) Reading aloud regularly with teacher feedback

b) Copying sentences from the board

c) Listening to recorded lectures

d) Writing vocabulary lists

Answer: a) Reading aloud regularly with teacher feedback

85. How can teachers foster listening comprehension?

a) By using audio resources followed by discussions

b) By focusing only on writing tasks

c) By ignoring oral language activities

d) By assigning only silent reading tasks

Answer: a) By using audio resources followed by discussions

86. What is the purpose of formative assessments in language learning?

a) To provide continuous feedback for improvement

b) To assign final grades only

c) To discourage independent learning

d) To avoid student participation

Answer: a) To provide continuous feedback for improvement

87. How does collaborative learning support language acquisition?

a) It promotes communication and teamwork

b) It discourages student interaction

c) It limits critical thinking

d) It focuses only on grammar rules

Answer: a) It promotes communication and teamwork

88. Which of the following helps students improve pronunciation?

a) Listening to native speakers and practicing aloud

b) Avoiding oral communication

c) Focusing only on written exercises

d) Memorizing grammar rules

Answer: a) Listening to native speakers and practicing aloud

89. What is the benefit of using multicultural texts in language teaching?

a) They reflect diverse experiences and promote inclusion

b) They discourage student engagement

c) They focus only on grammar practice

d) They limit language exposure

Answer: a) They reflect diverse experiences and promote inclusion

90. How can teachers support reluctant speakers?

a) By encouraging small group discussions

b) By avoiding oral tasks

c) By focusing only on written assessments

d) By giving only lecture-based lessons

Answer: a) By encouraging small group discussions

91. What is a benefit of using storytelling in language classes?

a) It enhances imagination and listening skills

b) It eliminates the need for writing

c) It focuses only on grammar correction

d) It discourages creativity

Answer: a) It enhances imagination and listening skills

92. How can teachers make language lessons more engaging?

a) By incorporating games and interactive activities

b) By using only textbook exercises

c) By giving long lectures without interaction

d) By avoiding group activities

Answer: a) By incorporating games and interactive activities

93. What is the role of open-ended questions in language learning?

a) They encourage critical thinking and expression

b) They limit student responses

c) They discourage class participation

d) They focus only on factual recall

Answer: a) They encourage critical thinking and expression

94. Which strategy promotes vocabulary retention?

a) Using new words in meaningful sentences

b) Memorizing word lists without practice

c) Avoiding conversations

d) Focusing only on spelling

Answer: a) Using new words in meaningful sentences

95. How can teachers evaluate listening skills effectively?

a) By asking students to summarize what they hear

b) By assigning grammar worksheets

c) By conducting spelling tests

d) By focusing only on written assignments

Answer: a) By asking students to summarize what they hear

96. What is a key feature of effective language teaching?

a) Creating opportunities for real-life communication

b) Focusing only on written work

c) Avoiding oral communication

d) Using only traditional lectures

Answer: a) Creating opportunities for real-life communication

97. How can teachers help students struggling with writing?

a) By providing writing prompts and feedback

b) By avoiding writing tasks

c) By focusing only on grammar drills

d) By assigning long reading assignments

Answer: a) By providing writing prompts and feedback

98. What is the purpose of role-play in language learning?

a) To simulate real-life situations for practice

b) To replace written assessments

c) To focus only on grammar correction

d) To avoid oral communication

Answer: a) To simulate real-life situations for practice

99. Which approach helps develop both listening and speaking skills?

a) Participating in interactive dialogues

b) Focusing only on textbook reading

c) Writing essays without discussion

d) Copying sentences from the board

Answer: a) Participating in interactive dialogues

100. How can teachers assess students' progress in language learning?

a) By using a variety of assessments, including oral and written tasks

b) By assigning only grammar worksheets

c) By focusing only on vocabulary tests

d) By avoiding feedback

Answer: a) By using a variety of assessments, including oral and written tasks

Chapter 2: Questions

101. How can teachers develop students' listening skills in a language classroom?

a) By using interactive listening activities, such as audio stories and discussions

b) By assigning only written tasks

c) By avoiding oral activities

d) By focusing only on vocabulary quizzes

Answer: a) By using interactive listening activities, such as audio stories and discussions

102. What role does feedback play in developing writing skills?

a) It guides students to improve structure and expression

b) It discourages creative writing

c) It focuses only on spelling errors

d) It avoids correcting student work

Answer: a) It guides students to improve structure and expression

103. Which strategy helps students expand their vocabulary?

a) Learning words through context and usage

b) Memorizing dictionaries without practice

c) Avoiding reading activities

d) Focusing only on spelling lists

Answer: a) Learning words through context and usage

104.What is the purpose of reading comprehension assessments?

a) To evaluate students' understanding of texts and their ability to make inferences

b) To test grammar rules exclusively

c) To assess spelling accuracy

d) To discourage independent reading

Answer: a) To evaluate students' understanding of texts and their ability to make inferences

105.How can teachers support students with diverse language abilities?

a) By using differentiated instruction and culturally relevant content

b) By assigning the same tasks to everyone

c) By focusing only on fluent speakers

d) By avoiding group activities

Answer: a) By using differentiated instruction and culturally relevant content

106.How can storytelling enhance language learning?

a) It fosters imagination, creativity, and listening skills

b) It eliminates the need for grammar practice

c) It focuses only on memorisation

d) It discourages student interaction

Answer: a) It fosters imagination, creativity, and listening skills

107.What is a crucial benefit of using real-world scenarios in language teaching?

a) It helps students apply language skills in practical contexts

b) It eliminates oral assessments

c) It focuses only on grammar correction

d) It limits student participation

Answer: a) It helps students apply language skills in practical contexts

108.How can teachers encourage reluctant readers?

a) By offering them books that match their interests and reading levels

b) By assigning only complex texts

c) By focusing only on grammar worksheets

d) By avoiding independent reading tasks

Answer: a) By offering them books that match their interests and reading levels

109.What is the role of pronunciation practice in language learning?

a) It helps students speak clearly and confidently

b) It discourages speaking activities

c) It focuses only on spelling patterns

d) It avoids interaction

Answer: a) It helps students speak clearly and confidently

110.How can teachers foster speaking confidence in students?

a) By providing opportunities for informal conversations and presentations

b) By focusing only on writing tasks

c) By avoiding oral activities

d) By limiting classroom discussions

Answer: a) By providing opportunities for informal conversations and presentations

111.What is an effective way to improve students' writing skills?

a) By assigning regular writing tasks with meaningful feedback

b) By avoiding creative writing activities

c) By focusing only on spelling and punctuation

d) By limiting feedback to final exams

Answer: a) By assigning regular writing tasks with meaningful feedback

112.How can group work enhance language learning?

a) It promotes teamwork, communication, and language practice

b) It limits student participation

c) It focuses only on individual tasks

d) It discourages collaborative efforts

Answer: a) It promotes teamwork, communication, and language practice

113.Which teaching strategy encourages critical thinking in language learning?

a) Using open-ended questions that require analysis

b) Memorizing vocabulary lists

c) Focusing only on grammar rules

d) Avoiding classroom discussions

Answer: a) Using open-ended questions that require analysis

114.How does continuous assessment benefit students?

a) It provides regular feedback for improvement throughout the course

b) It eliminates classroom participation

c) It focuses only on the final exam

d) It discourages independent learning

Answer: a) It provides regular feedback for improvement throughout the course

115.What is the benefit of integrating listening and speaking activities?

a) It improves communication skills and fluency

b) It limits vocabulary development

c) It discourages participation

d) It avoids real-world language use

Answer: a) It improves communication skills and fluency

116.How can teachers make grammar lessons more engaging?

a) By teaching grammar through games and interactive activities

b) By using only worksheets

c) By avoiding grammar discussions

d) By focusing solely on textbook exercises

Answer: a) By teaching grammar through games and interactive activities

117.What is the purpose of peer feedback in language learning?

a) It encourages students to reflect and learn from each other

b) It discourages collaboration

c) It eliminates teacher feedback

d) It focuses only on errors

Answer: a) It encourages students to reflect and learn from each other

118.How can teachers promote independent reading habits?

a) By allowing students to choose books based on their interests

b) By assigning only mandatory reading tasks

c) By discouraging choice in reading materials

d) By focusing only on textbook content

Answer: a) By allowing students to choose books based on their interests

119.What is a suitable way to assess listening comprehension?

a) Asking students to summarise the key points they heard

b) Giving only written grammar tests

c) Avoiding listening assessments

d) Conducting spelling drills

Answer: a) Asking students to summarise the key points they heard

120.How does collaborative learning improve language proficiency?

a) It encourages students to practice language through interaction

b) It eliminates independent study

c) It discourages critical thinking

d) It focuses only on individual performance

Answer: a) It encourages students to practice language through interaction

121.Which of the following activities improves vocabulary usage?

a) Encouraging students to use new words in conversations

b) Memorizing definitions without context

c) Focusing only on grammar correction

d) Avoiding oral language tasks

Answer: a) Encouraging students to use new words in conversations

122.How can role-play be used effectively in language classrooms?

a) By simulating real-life situations for practice

b) By replacing written assessments

c) By focusing only on grammar rules

d) By discouraging class participation

Answer: a) By simulating real-life situations for practice

123.What is the importance of remedial teaching in language learning?

a) It helps students overcome specific language challenges

b) It focuses only on high achievers

c) It eliminates classroom participation

d) It avoids feedback

Answer: a) It helps students overcome specific language challenges

124.How can teachers make reading comprehension tasks more engaging?

a) By selecting interesting and relevant texts

b) By assigning only factual texts

c) By focusing only on grammar rules

d) By avoiding interactive activities

Answer: a) By selecting interesting and relevant texts

125.What is the purpose of formative assessments?

a) To provide continuous feedback and guide improvement

b) To assign final grades only

c) To avoid giving feedback during the course

d) To discourage independent learning

Answer: a) To provide continuous feedback and guide improvement

126.How can teachers encourage writing fluency?

a) By providing regular writing opportunities with constructive feedback

b) By assigning only grammar worksheets

c) By avoiding creative tasks

d) By limiting writing activities

Answer: a) By providing regular writing opportunities with constructive feedback

127.What is the challenge of teaching language in a multilingual classroom?

a) Students have varying levels of proficiency

b) All students learn at the same pace

c) Language diversity simplifies instruction

d) There is no need for differentiated teaching

Answer: a) Students have varying levels of proficiency

128.Which strategy promotes active listening?

a) Engaging students in storytelling with follow-up questions

b) Focusing only on grammar drills

c) Avoiding oral discussions

d) Assigning only silent reading tasks

Answer: a) Engaging students in storytelling with follow-up questions

129.How does peer learning benefit students?

a) It encourages collaboration and shared responsibility

b) It discourages teamwork

c) It replaces teacher instruction entirely

d) It limits student engagement

Answer: a) It encourages collaboration and shared responsibility

130.What is the primary purpose of using poetry in language teaching?

a) To develop an appreciation for rhythm, imagery, and expression

b) To replace grammar exercises

c) To focus only on rhyme patterns

d) To discourage creative thought

Answer: a) To develop an appreciation for rhythm, imagery, and expression

131.What is an effective way to teach language through poetry?

a) By analysing imagery, tone, and themes

b) By focusing only on rhyme schemes

c) By avoiding discussions about meaning

d) By memorising the poem without understanding

Answer: a) By analysing imagery, tone, and themes

132.How can teachers help students struggling with pronunciation?

a) By using listening and repetition activities regularly

b) By focusing only on written tasks

c) By avoiding speaking activities

d) By assigning only reading assignments

Answer: a) By using listening and repetition activities regularly

133.What role does collaborative work play in language learning?

a) It encourages students to practice speaking and listening in groups

b) It limits individual accountability

c) It discourages critical thinking

d) It replaces independent learning

Answer: a) It encourages students to practice speaking and listening in groups

134.Which strategy helps improve listening comprehension?

a) Engaging students in interactive listening tasks, such as interviews or podcasts

b) Focusing only on grammar exercises

c) Avoiding oral assessments

d) Conducting silent reading sessions only

Answer: a) Engaging students in interactive listening tasks, such as interviews or podcasts

135.How does scaffolding benefit language learners?

a) It provides support that gradually decreases as learners gain proficiency

b) It eliminates the need for independent work

c) It discourages student autonomy

d) It focuses only on written language

Answer: a) It provides support that gradually decreases as learners gain proficiency

136.How can teachers motivate reluctant writers?

a) By providing creative and meaningful writing prompts

b) By focusing only on handwriting

c) By avoiding feedback

d) By assigning only factual writing tasks

Answer: a) By providing creative and meaningful writing prompts

137.What is the primary purpose of remedial teaching in language development?

a) To address students' specific challenges and fill learning gaps

b) To teach advanced language concepts

c) To replace regular classroom teaching

d) To discourage individual feedback

Answer: a) To address students' specific challenges and fill learning gaps

138.What is the benefit of using culturally relevant materials in language teaching?

a) They make learning more relatable and inclusive for students

b) They eliminate the need for grammar instruction

c) They limit classroom participation

d) They discourage group activities

Answer: a) They make learning more relatable and inclusive for students

139.How does peer feedback enhance language learning?

a) It allows students to reflect on their own and others' work

b) It replaces teacher feedback entirely

c) It focuses only on mistakes

d) It discourages collaboration

Answer: a) It allows students to reflect on their own and others' work

140. Which method encourages students to build reading fluency?

a) Reading aloud regularly with guidance from the teacher

b) Writing essays without reading aloud

c) Focusing only on spelling drills

d) Conducting silent reading without discussion

Answer: a) Reading aloud regularly with guidance from the teacher

141. What is an essential goal of continuous assessment in language learning?

a) To provide regular feedback and monitor progress

b) To conduct only final exams

c) To limit feedback to grammar corrections

d) To focus only on grades

Answer: a) To provide regular feedback and monitor progress

142. How can teachers promote listening comprehension in students?

a) By encouraging active listening through discussions after audio activities

b) By focusing only on reading skills

c) By avoiding oral activities

d) By assigning only vocabulary lists

Answer: a) By encouraging active listening through discussions after audio activities

143. What is the purpose of role-play in language classes?

a) To help students practice real-life communication skills

b) To replace writing activities

c) To focus only on grammar drills

d) To avoid oral communication

Answer: a) To help students practice real-life communication skills

144. Which activity promotes vocabulary retention?

a) Using new words actively in conversations

b) Memorizing word lists without practice

c) Focusing only on grammar rules

d) Ignoring unfamiliar words

Answer: a) Using new words actively in conversations

145.How does group discussion benefit language learners?

a) It encourages speaking, listening, and critical thinking skills

b) It discourages teamwork

c) It eliminates the need for individual assessments

d) It focuses only on competition

Answer: a) It encourages speaking, listening, and critical thinking skills

146.What is a crucial benefit of formative assessments in language development?

a) They provide timely feedback to guide improvement

b) They focus only on final grades

c) They discourage classroom participation

d) They replace all other assessments

Answer: a) They provide timely feedback to guide improvement

147.How can teachers create an inclusive language classroom?

a) By acknowledging and incorporating students' diverse backgrounds

b) By treating all students identically

c) By focusing only on advanced learners

d) By avoiding culturally relevant content

Answer: a) By acknowledging and incorporating students' diverse backgrounds

148.What role does creative writing play in language development?

a) It encourages imagination and helps improve expression

b) It focuses only on grammar accuracy

c) It discourages creativity

d) It replaces reading comprehension activities

Answer: a) It encourages imagination and helps improve expression

149.Which strategy helps students develop pronunciation skills?

a) Listening to native speakers and practising aloud

b) Focusing only on spelling patterns

c) Avoiding oral communication

d) Memorizing vocabulary lists

Answer: a) Listening to native speakers and practising aloud

150.How can teachers support students with language learning difficulties?

a) By providing individualised instruction and feedback

b) By assigning the same tasks to everyone

c) By focusing only on written assignments

d) By avoiding group activities

Answer: a) By providing individualised instruction and feedback

151.Which strategy helps students improve their speaking fluency?

a) Engaging in regular conversations and presentations

b) Memorizing vocabulary lists without usage

c) Focusing only on written grammar exercises

d) Avoiding oral communication activities

Answer: a) Engaging in regular conversations and presentations

152.How can teachers promote critical thinking through reading activities?

a) By asking students to analyse and infer meanings from texts

b) By focusing only on literal comprehension

c) By discouraging questioning

d) By assigning only factual recall questions

Answer: a) By asking students to analyse and infer meanings from texts

153.What is the role of listening activities in language learning?

a) To develop comprehension, pronunciation, and attention skills

b) To avoid oral interaction

c) To focus only on written work

d) To replace reading activities

Answer: a) To develop comprehension, pronunciation, and attention skills

154.How can teachers foster students' motivation in language learning?

a) By connecting learning to students' interests and real-life contexts

b) By assigning only repetitive tasks

c) By avoiding group activities

d) By limiting creative tasks

Answer: a) By connecting learning to students' interests and real-life contexts

155.Which method helps students develop listening comprehension skills?

a) Listening to dialogues and summarising key points

b) Writing essays without discussion

c) Focusing only on textbook activities

d) Avoiding oral assessments

Answer: a) Listening to dialogues and summarising key points

156.How can teachers encourage reluctant speakers?

a) By creating a supportive environment with small group discussions

b) By focusing only on written assignments

c) By discouraging participation in oral activities

d) By assigning only grammar drills

Answer: a) By creating a supportive environment with small group discussions

157.What is the benefit of integrating language skills in lessons?

a) It provides a balanced approach to speaking, listening, reading, and writing

b) It focuses only on individual skills

c) It discourages classroom interaction

d) It replaces formative assessments

Answer: a) It provides a balanced approach to speaking, listening, reading, and writing

158.How can teachers assess students' language comprehension effectively?

a) By using a mix of oral, written, and listening assessments

b) By focusing only on grammar tests

c) By assigning only multiple-choice questions

d) By avoiding oral assessments

Answer: a) By using a mix of oral, written, and listening assessments

159.What is the role of group activities in language learning?

a) To encourage teamwork, communication, and shared learning

b) To focus only on individual tasks

c) To limit classroom participation

d) To discourage collaboration

Answer: a) To encourage teamwork, communication, and shared learning

160.How does peer feedback enhance learning?

a) It provides new perspectives and encourages self-reflection

b) It discourages participation

c) It replaces all teacher feedback

d) It focuses only on mistakes

Answer: a) It provides new perspectives and encourages self-reflection

161.Which teaching strategy promotes vocabulary retention?

a) Using new words in meaningful contexts and conversations

b) Memorizing word lists without usage

c) Focusing only on definitions

d) Ignoring unknown words

Answer: a) Using new words in meaningful contexts and conversations

162.What is the purpose of formative assessments?

a) To provide timely feedback that guides students toward improvement

b) To assign final grades only

c) To discourage creativity in tasks

d) To focus only on testing knowledge

Answer: a) To provide timely feedback that guides students toward improvement

163.How can teachers create an inclusive language classroom?

a) By respecting and integrating students' diverse cultural backgrounds

b) By treating all students the same way without adaptation

c) By ignoring diversity in the classroom

d) By focusing only on written assessments

Answer: a) By respecting and integrating students' diverse cultural backgrounds

164.What is the benefit of role-play in language teaching?

a) It provides opportunities to practice communication in realistic situations

b) It eliminates the need for written assessments

c) It focuses only on pronunciation drills

d) It discourages class participation

Answer: a) It provides opportunities to practice communication in realistic situations

165.How can teachers help students struggling with writing?

a) By offering structured prompts and giving constructive feedback

b) By avoiding writing tasks

c) By assigning only grammar worksheets

d) By limiting feedback to final assessments

Answer: a) By offering structured prompts and giving constructive feedback

166.How can teachers encourage independent reading?

a) By allowing students to choose books that interest them

b) By assigning only mandatory reading lists

c) By focusing only on textbook content

d) By avoiding discussions about books

Answer: a) By allowing students to choose books that interest them

167.Which activity promotes fluency in reading?

a) Regular reading aloud with guidance and feedback

b) Memorizing vocabulary without practice

c) Avoiding oral reading activities

d) Focusing only on silent reading

Answer: a) Regular reading aloud with guidance and feedback

168.How can teachers improve listening comprehension?

a) By engaging students in discussions after audio-based activities

b) By assigning only written assessments

c) By avoiding oral interaction

d) By focusing only on grammar correction

Answer: a) By engaging students in discussions after audio-based activities

169.What is the benefit of project-based language learning?

a) It encourages the application of language skills in real-world contexts

b) It eliminates collaboration

c) It focuses only on grammar rules

d) It discourages participation

Answer: a) It encourages the application of language skills in real-world contexts

170.How can teachers foster creativity in language learning?

a) By providing opportunities for creative writing and expression

b) By avoiding imaginative tasks

c) By focusing only on factual recall

d) By limiting storytelling activities

Answer: a) By providing opportunities for creative writing and expression

171.Which technique helps develop pronunciation skills?

a) Listening to and imitating native speakers

b) Memorizing grammar rules

c) Avoiding oral communication

d) Conducting only spelling tests

Answer: a) Listening to and imitating native speakers

172.How can teachers support students with language difficulties?

a) By providing tailored instruction and regular feedback

b) By assigning identical tasks to everyone

c) By avoiding individualised support

d) By focusing only on advanced students

Answer: a) By providing tailored instruction and regular feedback

173.What is the role of input in language learning?

a) To guide students in refining their skills and understanding

b) To discourage participation

c) To replace assessments

d) To focus only on grades

Answer: a) To guide students in refining their skills and understanding

174.How can teachers promote collaborative learning?

a) By encouraging teamwork through group activities and discussions

b) By focusing only on individual work

c) By limiting classroom interaction

d) By discouraging group efforts

Answer: a) By encouraging teamwork through group activities and discussions

175.What is a crucial feature of inclusive education in language classrooms?

a) Valuing and addressing the needs of all students

b) Treating all students the same without adaptation

c) Focusing only on high achievers

d) Avoiding discussions about diversity

Answer: a) Valuing and addressing the needs of all students

176.How can teachers foster speaking confidence?

a) By creating opportunities for informal conversations and presentations

b) By avoiding oral tasks

c) By focusing only on grammar corrections

d) By limiting student interaction

Answer: a) By creating opportunities for informal conversations and presentations

177.What is the purpose of storytelling in language learning?

a) To enhance imagination, listening skills, and language usage

b) To focus only on grammar

c) To replace written assessments

d) To discourage participation

Answer: a) To enhance imagination, listening skills, and language usage

178.How can teachers assess reading comprehension effectively?

a) By asking questions about main ideas, themes, and inferences

b) By focusing only on vocabulary tests

c) By avoiding discussions about the text

d) By assigning only spelling exercises

Answer: a) By asking questions about main ideas, themes, and inferences

179.What is the goal of language acquisition activities?

a) To develop fluency through meaningful interactions

b) To focus only on grammar rules

c) To discourage oral communication

d) To limit vocabulary development

Answer: a) To develop fluency through meaningful interactions

180.Which approach helps develop listening and speaking skills simultaneously?

a) Engaging students in conversations and role-play

b) Assigning only written tasks

c) Avoiding oral communication activities

d) Focusing only on silent reading

Answer: a) Engaging students in conversations and role-play

181.How can teachers encourage reluctant readers?

a) By introducing books that match their interests and reading levels

b) By assigning only challenging and complex texts

c) By avoiding independent reading activities

d) By limiting discussions about books

Answer: a) By introducing books that match their interests and reading levels

182.What is the purpose of remedial teaching in language development?

a) To address specific challenges faced by struggling students

b) To focus only on grammar rules

c) To eliminate classroom discussions

d) To assign additional homework

Answer: a) To address specific challenges faced by struggling students

183.How can teachers promote vocabulary development?

a) By encouraging students to use new words in conversations and writing

b) By focusing only on memorising word lists

c) By assigning repetitive grammar exercises

d) By avoiding vocabulary-related tasks

Answer: a) By encouraging students to use new words in conversations and writing

184.Which activity best supports listening comprehension?

a) Listening to an audio clip and answering related questions

b) Assigning only written grammar tasks

c) Focusing only on silent reading activities

d) Avoiding audio-based activities

Answer: a) Listening to an audio clip and answering related questions

185.What role does continuous assessment play in language learning?

a) It helps track progress and provides regular feedback

b) It focuses only on the final exam

c) It discourages student participation

d) It eliminates the need for feedback

Answer: a) It helps track progress and provides regular feedback

186.How can teachers develop students' writing skills?

a) By assigning meaningful writing prompts and providing feedback

b) By avoiding creative writing tasks

c) By focusing only on spelling corrections

d) By limiting writing to textbook-based tasks

Answer: a) By assigning meaningful writing prompts and providing feedback

187.What is the benefit of peer learning in language development?

a) It promotes collaboration and shared responsibility

b) It eliminates individual accountability

c) It discourages classroom participation

d) It replaces all teacher instruction

Answer: a) It promotes collaboration and shared responsibility

188.How can teachers enhance pronunciation skills in students?

a) By using repetition and exposure to native speakers

b) By avoiding spoken language practice

c) By focusing only on spelling drills

d) By assigning only written work

Answer: a) By using repetition and exposure to native speakers

189.What is the primary purpose of storytelling in language classes?

a) To enhance listening, comprehension, and imagination

b) To replace grammar instruction

c) To discourage student interaction

d) To avoid oral language activities

Answer: a) To enhance listening, comprehension, and imagination

190.How can teachers promote critical thinking through reading?

a) By asking open-ended questions and encouraging analysis

b) By focusing only on memorization

c) By discouraging student inquiry

d) By limiting discussions about texts

Answer: a) By asking open-ended questions and encouraging analysis

191.Which activity supports the development of speaking skills?

a) Group discussions and role-plays

b) Silent reading activities

c) Memorizing spelling lists

d) Writing only grammar-based essays

Answer: a) Group discussions and role-plays

192.How does inclusive education benefit language learners?

a) It ensures all students have access to meaningful learning experiences

b) It focuses only on high achievers

c) It avoids accommodating diverse needs

d) It eliminates collaborative activities

Answer: a) It ensures all students have access to meaningful learning experiences

193.What is the purpose of formative assessments in language learning?

a) To provide ongoing feedback to improve student performance

b) To focus only on end-of-term exams

c) To discourage student participation

d) To assign final grades without feedback

Answer: a) To provide ongoing feedback to improve student performance

194.How can teachers address students' language learning challenges?

a) By offering individualized support and differentiated instruction

b) By assigning identical tasks to all students

c) By focusing only on advanced learners

d) By avoiding feedback

Answer: a) By offering individualized support and differentiated instruction

195.What is the role of feedback in developing writing skills?

a) It helps students refine their ideas and structure

b) It discourages student creativity

c) It focuses only on errors

d) It eliminates the need for revisions

Answer: a) It helps students refine their ideas and structure

196.How can teachers promote active listening in students?

a) By engaging them in discussions about what they hear

b) By focusing only on silent reading tasks

c) By avoiding group activities

d) By assigning only grammar worksheets

Answer: a) By engaging them in discussions about what they hear

197.What is the benefit of using culturally diverse texts in language learning?

a) They foster inclusion and make learning relatable

b) They discourage student participation

c) They eliminate critical thinking tasks

d) They replace traditional grammar lessons

Answer: a) They foster inclusion and make learning relatable

198.Which activity helps build fluency in spoken language?

a) Regular conversations and oral presentations

b) Silent reading sessions

c) Memorizing spelling rules

d) Writing essays without oral practice

Answer: a) Regular conversations and oral presentations

199.How can teachers support reluctant speakers in the classroom?

a) By creating a safe space for informal conversations and presentations

b) By avoiding spoken language activities

c) By focusing only on written assessments

d) By assigning only textbook-based tasks

Answer: a) By creating a safe space for informal conversations and presentations

200. What is the primary goal of remedial teaching in language learning?

a) To help students overcome learning difficulties and fill gaps

b) To teach advanced grammar concepts

c) To replace classroom instruction

d) To avoid individualized feedback

Answer: a) To help students overcome learning difficulties and fill gaps

9 789349 018556

Printed at Repro India Ltd.